Boy Tales of Childhood Discussion and Writing Unit Plan

Timothy R. Baldwin

Published by Timothy R. Baldwin, 2024.

BOY TALES OF CHILDHOOD DISCUSSION AND WRITING UNIT PLAN

First edition. March 28, 2024.

Copyright © 2024 Timothy R. Baldwin.

ISBN: 979-8224917730

Written by Timothy R. Baldwin.

Also by Timothy R. Baldwin

The Unwanted Guest and Other Short Thrillers
Boy Tales of Childhood Discussion and Writing Unit Plan

Watch for more at www.timothyrbaldwin.com.

Table of Contents

About the Unit Plan 1

Desired Results (TR) 4

Reading and Assignment Guide (SR) 9

Unit Project Overview (SR) 13

Starting Point to Mrs. Pratchett's Revenge (TR) 16

Going to Norway to A Visit to the Doctor (TR) 20

First Day to Homesickness (TR) 23

BCR Essay Characterization/Figurative Language (SR) ... 26

A Drive in the Motor Car to Little Ellis and the Boil (TR) 28

Focused Class Discussion on A Drive in the Motor Car to Little Ellis and the Boil (SR) 30

Goat's Tobacco (TR) 33

BCR Essay Author's Style (SR) 36

Midway Theme Assignment (SR) 38

Theme BCR (SR) 41

Getting dressed for the big school, Boazers, The Headmaster, Chocolates (TR) 43

Point of View, Memory Details, Reflective Details (SR) ... 45

Point of View BCR (SR) 48

Corkers, Fagging, Games and photography, Goodbye school (TR) 50

Corkers to Goodbye School Discussion Preparation (SR) 52

Plot Comparison (SR) 56

About the Unit Plan

This unit plan is designed to promote student discussion within the classroom.

Each of the teacher resource (TR) pages contains question ideas to be used to help a teacher facilitate a class discussion in the stages of Initial Understanding, Developing Ideas, Learning from the Text, and Critical Stance. When facilitating a classroom discussion, it is important to let the students do most of the talking. Therefore, a discussion should begin with the students' "wonderings" about the text and be followed by the responses of other students.

The Reading and Assignment Guide is designed so that students are required to respond to the text during and after they have finished the assigned reading. It is important to remind the students that their "Wonder Questions" should not be "find out" questions but should be "figure out" questions. In other words, the aim of their questions is to promote discussion that begins with the students. In addition to the 5 Wonder Questions, the students are also required to identify the author's use of literary devices within the novel. It is recommended that the teacher model how to find these elements within the text prior to sending the students home to read.

Students should also be reminded to list and explain the 3 most important events within each section of reading. Responses for these will vary.

The assessment pieces – BCR (Brief Constructed Response) Essays and the final plot analysis – can be used as formative or summative assessments depending on how much prior knowledge a class may have had with the specific skill being assessed. It is likely that students will have a harder time with Point of View and evaluating the author's style of writing. Analyzing the author's use of figurative language to create a character and identifying and analyzing recurring themes may become easier for your students. Again, it depends upon how much practice the students have had with applying the terminology to literary analysis.

Finally, this unit plan promotes students' original thoughts and ideas in response to the literature being studied in class. Therefore, the excessive use of worksheets has only been limited to pieces for assessment. As a result, a spiral or composition notebook is recommended for use with this unit plan. This greatly reduces the number of pieces of paper students have to keep track of and allows them to focus on reading and enjoying the novel.

Final Thoughts:

This unit plan is a product of teaching <u>Boy, Tales of Childhood</u> for the third year. Because so much emphasis was placed on discussion, which engaged the students' interest, no student complained about the amount of reading, the amount of work, or the content of the novel itself. Generally, every student experienced some degree of enjoyment as they read the novel and engaged in the discussion.

For more ideas on how to promote quality discussion in your classroom, I recommend *Building Literacy through Classroom Discussion* by Mary Adler and Eija Rougle. I am also willing to provide insight into how this worked in my classroom.

Sincerely,

Timothy Baldwin

Desired Results (TR)

Established Goals:

Students will be able to analyze elements of narrative narrative to facilitate understanding and interpretation: character, plot, theme, author's craft, mood, and tone.

Students will be able to identify and analyze the author's craft to imitate the writing style in their own work.

Understandings:

Students will understand that...

- Point of view affects the way the story is told.
- Figurative Language choices can be used within a narrative to exaggerate experiences and characters.
- Dahl's novel is broken up into many different plots, which can be analyzed as a self-contained unit.
- How nonlinear plot structures can be used to tell a story that is thematic in nature.

Essential Questions:

- How does Dahl's point of view as a child and point of view as an adult affect the way he tells each story?
- How does Dahl use figurative language for characterization?
- How does each smaller story (plot) relate to Dahl's entire story as a child and as a student?
- How does the nonlinear plot structure support this novel's theme(s)?

Students will know...

- How to identify and analyze point of view
- How to identify and analyze figurative language

- How to evaluate the effectiveness of word choice
- How to identify and analyze the plot within the stories Dahl tells.
- How to analyze and evaluate the use of a non-linear plot structure.

Students will be able to...
- Analyze point of view
- Analyze figurative language
- Evaluate the use of figurative language
- Evaluate the use of a non-linear plot structure
- Imitate the author's craft

Assessment Evidence

PERFORMANCE TASKS: *(SUMMATIVE)*

Create a journal/diary consisting of at least 8 entries about your life. Entries should not contain boring details but focus on the most memorable moments in your life – exciting, enjoyable, painful, and humiliating. Journal/diary should contain sketches, figurative language to create a character, elements of point of view reflective in nature, narrative in nature (I/you pronouns), and specific and precise word choice to create the experiences and character. The journal/diary should be arranged thematically with some sense of chronological order.

OTHER EVIDENCE: *(FORMATIVE)*

1. BCR: Identify a moment in the novel where Dahl uses point of view (as a child and as an adult) to tell the story and reflect upon it. Explain the effect that these two perspectives have on the story.

2. BCR: Analyze Dahl's use of figurative language for characterization (choose an adult).

3. BCR: Evaluate the effectiveness of Dahl's writing style in telling his story(ies).

4. BCR: Identify and explain one recurring theme in the novel. In your explanation, include what the reader can learn about life through Dahl's novel.

Learning Plan

ACTIVE READING: Focused note-taking on each section of reading.

GROUP AND SOLO WORK: In class and at home activities related to "students will know how."

- Analysis of plot structure
- Analysis of characterization
- Identification and analysis of point of view
- Evaluate word choice/figurative language. Analysis of how events and mini-stories in the novel relate to one another

The first half of the novel should be a lot of guided practice and modeling with opportunities for group work to practice the skills. The novel's second half should focus on pair work with the BCRs as an at-home assignment.

READING SECTIONS

1. *Starting point*, pgs. 11-23 (together in class)
2. *Llandaff Cathedral School*, pgs. 27-71
- pgs. 27-52
- pgs. 53-71
3. *St Peter's*, pgs. 75-132
- pgs. 75-98
- pgs. 99-126
4. pgs. 127-132 (together in class)
5. *Repton and Shell*, pgs. 135-176

- Pgs. 135-149
- Pgs. 150-176

Reading and Assignment Guide (SR)

This novel unit is designed to promote classroom discussion to aid in your understanding of what you are reading each night. While your teacher will facilitate classroom discussions of the literature, the discussion will depend upon you doing the reading each night and completing the activity portion of the assignment.

1. Date ___________: **In class:** Read pgs. 11-23. **Homework**: Read pgs. 27-52

- **Boy, pgs. 27-52, ACTIVE READING:** Write five wonder questions, list three examples of **CONFLICT**, and identify and explain three of the most important events in the section.

2. Date ___________: **In class:** Discuss pgs. 27-52. **Homework:** Read pgs. 53-71

- **Boy, pgs. 53-71, ACTIVE READING:** Write five wonder questions, list three examples of **SENSORY LANGUAGE**, and identify and explain three of the most important events in the section.

3. Date ___________: **In class:** Discuss pgs. 53-71. **Homework:** Begin reading pgs. 75-98

- **Boy, pgs. 75-98, ACTIVE READING:** Write five wonder questions, list three examples of **CHARACTERIZATION**, and identify and explain three of the most important events in the section.

4. Date ___________: **In class:** Discuss pgs. 75-98. **Homework:** Figurative Language to Create Character BCR

5. Date ___________: In class: Begin reading pgs. 99-126 Homework: Read pgs. 99-126

- Boy, pgs. 99-126, ACTIVE READING: Write five wonder questions, list three examples of CLIMAX, and identify and explain three of the most important events in the section.

6. Date ___________: In class: Discuss pgs. 99-126. Homework: Read pgs. 127-132

- Boy, pgs. 127-132, ACTIVE READING: Write five wonder questions, list three examples of EXAGERATION, and identify and explain three of the most important events in the section.

7. Date ___________: In class: Discuss pgs. 127-132. Homework: Finish Author's Style BCR

8. Date ___________: In class: Discuss Themes & BCR. Homework: Read pgs. 135-149.

- Boy, pgs. 135-149, ACTIVE READING: Write five wonder questions, list three examples of REFLECTIVE DETAILS, and identify and explain three of the most important events in the section.

9. Date ___________: In class: Discuss pgs. 135-149. Point of View Worksheet & BCR. Homework: Finish Point of View BCR

10. Date ___________: In class: Begin Reading pgs. 150-176. Homework: Finish Reading pgs. 150-176

- Boy, pgs. 150-176, ACTIVE READING: Write five wonder questions, list ONE example of A SIGNIFICANT CHARACTER RELATIONSHIP FROM THE ENTIRE STORY, and identify and explain three of the most important events in the section.

11. □ Date ___________: In class: Discuss pgs. 150-176.

12. Date ___________: Plot Review. Compare the plot organization in two chapters of the novel. Homework: Finish Plot Review.

Unit Project Overview (SR)

Create a journal/diary consisting of at least 8 entries about your life. Each entry should be at least a page long and should not contain boring details but focus on the most memorable moments in your life – exciting, enjoyable, painful, and humiliating. The journal/diary should contain sketches, figurative language to create a character, elements of point of view-reflective in nature, narrative in nature (/You pronouns), and specific and precise word choice to create the experiences and characters. The journal/diary should be arranged thematically with some sense of chronological order.

SCORE SHEET

1. 8 entries, each a page in length /8 pts
2. Each of the eight entries focuses on the most memorable moments – exciting, enjoyable, painful, and humiliating. /8 pts
3. Four of the eight entries contain sketches /4 pts
4. Four examples of **figurative language** to create a character are highlighted. /4 pts
5. Entries are **narrative** and **reflective** /8 pts
6. All eight entries contain specific and precise word choice /8 pts
7. Memories are arranged **thematically** /3 pts
8. Memories are arranged **chronologically** /3 pts
9. Conventions – grammar, spelling, and punctuation (minus 1 pt for every 4 errors) /4 pts

________/50 pts

Starting Point to Mrs. Pratchett's Revenge (TR)

Page Numbers/Chapters:
- *Starting Point, Kindergarten*; pgs.11-23
- *Llandaff Cathedral School (The Bicycle and the Sweet Shop, The Great Mouse Plot, Mr. Coombes, Mrs. Pratchett's Revenge, Going to Norway to A Visit to the Doctor (TR)*, pgs. 27-52

INITIAL UNDERSTANDING:
- Students share and discuss.
- Wonder Questions
- Big 6
- What is this story about?

LEARNING FROM THE TEXT:
- Themes, social issues, and how the story changes the reader's perspective.
- What do we learn about Roald Dahl's world from his family background to when he was seven?
- Are there any social problems that may have been around during this time?
- Were all people treated fairly?
- What theme or themes seem to be occurring? How might this section relate to the idea of Learning From Experience: Knowing Who You Are or Moments of Discovery?

DEVELOPING IDEAS:

Larger ideas include the big picture, what is happening, why, and how characters act.
- What kind of person is Dahl's mother?

- Why do you think Dahl remembered the boy on the bicycle? (pg. 28)

- Why do you think Dahl may have remembered Thwaites over his other friends?

- Why does Dahl expect the reader to understand that he and his friends had "it in for Mrs. Pratchett in a big way"?

- What do you think made this part of the story memorable for Dahl?

- What kind of children were Dahl and his friends in this chapter?

- What kind of people are Mrs. Pratchett and Mr. Coombes?

TAKING A CRITICAL STANCE:

Text's construction, language, effect on the reader, connections to other texts, perspective, writer's choice, powerful language, and metaphors.

- What did you think of the way Dahl describes Mrs. Pratchet? (pg. 33, 43)

- What did you think of Dahl's "The Great Mouse Plot" description? How does he use language to build suspense and excitement?

- How effective is Dahl's use of foreshadowing to build suspense? (pg. 39)

- What did you think of the way Dahl describes Mr.

- Coombes? (pg. 41)

- Contrast the image of Mrs. Pratchet and Mr.

- Coombes. (pg. 42)

- How effective is Dahl at conveying his building internal conflict? (pg. 41-45)

• Do you think *Mrs. Pratchet's Revenge* was a realistic telling? To what extent? Why or why not?

• Do you think Dahl's negative experience toward this memory may have skewed the story?

Conflict

• Dahl vs. Mrs. Pratchett

• Dahl vs. Mr. Coombes

• Dahl vs. himself – the decision to hide the mouse in the gobstopper dish, fear of getting caught.

Going to Norway to A Visit to the Doctor (TR)

Page Numbers/Chapters:

Pgs. 53-71, *Going to Norway, The Magic Island, A Visit to the Doctor*

INITIAL UNDERSTANDING:
- Students share and discuss.
- Wonder Questions
- Big 6
- What is this story about?

LEARNING FROM THE TEXT:

Themes, social issues, how the story changes the reader's perspective.

- What does Dahl want the reader to understand about Norwegian culture and society? *(Going to Norway)*
- What ideas about life may Dahl have wanted to convey to the reader? Consider his statement: *I tell you, my friends, those were the days.* (pg. 67)
- What may have Dahl wanted the reader to understand about medicine when he was a child? (pg. 71)

DEVELOPING IDEAS:

Larger ideas, the big picture, what is happening, why it's happening, why and how characters act and do things

- Based on what he has told us about some things his mother has done so far, how does Dahl view his mother?
- What do you think are significant about Dahl's images of his grandparents? (pgs.55 & 56)

- Why might the feast at his grandparents' house be so important for Dahl's memory?

- Based on his descriptions in *The Magic Island*, how does Dahl feel toward this destination? What examples can you find to support your ideas?

- Why do you think Dahl may have been able to describe the long, shiny steel instrument perfectly? (p 69)

TAKING A CRITICAL STANCE:

Text's construction, language, effect on the reader, connections to other texts, perspective, writer's choice, powerful language, metaphors

- Unlike the previous section of this book, which was about *The Great Mouse Plot* and Dahl's conflicts with Mrs. Pratchett and Mr. Coombes, there is no actual "story," but there are a lot of images. Why do you think Dahl may have chosen to write this portion without any conflicts? What do you think he may have been trying to convey to the reader about his experience?

- If you were to identify a story in this section, where would it be? Does it contain all of the elements of the plot? Identify them. (*A Visit to the Doctor*)

- Examine the sensory language you identified in the story. How effective was Dahl at creating some of those images for the reader? How does the reader get a sense of his feelings toward these people, events, and experiences?

Sensory Language:
- Grandparents, pg. 55 & 56
- Dinner feast, pg. 57
- *The Magic Island,* pg. 61
- Description of the long shiny steel instrument, pg. 69

First Day to Homesickness (TR)

Page Numbers/Chapters

Pages 75-98, *First Day, Writing Home, Homesick*

INITIAL UNDERSTANDING:

- Students share and discuss.
- Wonder Questions
- Big 6
- What is this story about?

LEARNING FROM THE TEXT:

Themes, social issues, how the story changes the reader's perspective.

What does Roald Dahl teach us about the nature of boarding schools during his time?

DEVELOPING IDEAS:

Larger ideas, the big picture, what is happening, why it's happening, why and how characters act and do things

- Based on what you know about the young Roald, what do you think he had in his tuck box? Explain. (pg. 76)
- What kind of person is the headmaster of
- St. Peter's School? (pg. 78)
- What kind of relationship did Roald Dahl have with his mother when he was a child?
- *(Writing Home, pg. 80)*
- How well do you think the boys at St. Peter's school learned to spell? (pg. 83)
- Why does Dahl seem only to remember that the matron was "a fair-haired woman with a bosom" (pg. 85)? Why do you

think the matron chose to work at St. Peter's School? How close is Dr. Dunbar to the family?

- How do you know? (pg. 97)

TAKING A CRITICAL STANCE:

Text's construction, language, effect on the reader, connections to other texts, perspective, writer's choice, powerful language, metaphors

- Dahl writes the chapter, *Writing Home*, like many other chapters. He mentions something in writing which reminds him of a later experience. What does this tell us about his style of writing?

- What was your reaction to the story about what the Matron did to Tweedie? What imagery did Dahl use to help the reader visualize the experience? (pg. 90)

Figurative Language

- The headmaster of St. Peter's School is described as a giant shark (pgs.78 & 79)

- Matron would prowl the corridor like a panther (pg. 87).

BCR Essay Characterization/ Figurative Language (SR)

Boy, Tales of Childhood, pp 75-98

BCR Essay Characterization/Figurative Language

Explain how Dahl uses figurative language to characterize. Use examples and details from the text to support your response.

BCR Grading Scale

20 – Answer the question with two clear, relevant examples, and a meaningful extension/explanation.

17– Answer the question with two clear, relevant examples and a weak extension/explanation.

15– Answer the question with two clear, relevant examples.

13 – Answer the question with one clear, relevant example.

11– Answer the question

0– Response is completely incorrect, irrelevant to the question, or missing

A Drive in the Motor Car to Little Ellis and the Boil (TR)

Page Numbers/Chapters

Pages 99-126, *A Drive in the Motor Car, Captain Hardcastle, Little Ellis, and the boil*

INITIAL UNDERSTANDING:

- Students share and discuss.
- Wonder Questions
- Big 6
- What is this story about?

LEARNING FROM THE TEXT:

Themes, social issues, how the story changes the reader's perspective.

- What does the chapter, *A Drive in the Motor Car*, teach us about how society understood automobiles at the time?

- What do you think of how children are treated at St. Peter's compared to your school? Would you still like to go to an English boarding school?

DEVELOPING IDEAS:

Larger ideas, the big picture, what is happening, why it's happening, why and how characters act and do things

- How many automobile accidents were there in 1925? (pg. 101)

- Why would a driving instructor only spend two and a half hours instructing a new driver and not teach the new driver to drive backward? (pg. 104)

- If the egg seller was impatient, why didn't he bother to help move the automobile? (pg. 104)

• Why did Capt. Hardcastle have it in for young Roald? (pg. 110)

TAKING A CRITICAL STANCE:

Text's construction, language, effect on the reader, connections to other texts, perspective, writer's choice, powerful language, metaphors

• What were your impressions of Captain Hardcastle's descriptions on pages 108 to 109? What did you think of the boys' conclusions about him?

• What were your impressions of the sounds one would hear in prep? (pg. 113)

• What did you think about the system of stars and stripes and the consequences? (pg. 116)

• What were your impressions of how the headmaster dealt with the punishment? (pg. 120)

• What were your impressions of how the doctor treated Ellis' boil? (pg. 125)

Climax:

• Car crash, pg. 103
• The reception of the stripe, pg. 116
• The sixth stroke of the cane, pg. 121

Focused Class Discussion on A Drive in the Motor Car to Little Ellis and the Boil (SR)

Boy, pgs.99-126, Classwork

Directions to Teacher:

This assignment is divided into three sections of reading. Some options for assigning the work are jigsaw fashion or small group discussions with a designated spokesperson.

GROUP 1:

- Reread pages 100-103
    - Identify the CLIMAX in this section
    - What language choices to Roald

CRITICAL STANCE RESPONSE

What were your impressions of how Captain Hardcastle is described on pages 108 to 109? What did you think of the boys' conclusions of Captain Hardcastle? Use examples from the text to support your impressions.

LEARNING FROM THE TEXT RESPONSE

What does the chapter, A Drive in the Motor Car, teach us about how society understood automobiles at the time? Use examples from the text to support your impressions.

———

GROUP 2:

- Reread pages 113-116

- Identify the CLIMAX in this section
- What language choices does Roald Dahl make to lead to this climactic moment?

CRITICAL STANCE RESPONSE

What were your impressions of the sounds one would hear in prep? (pg. 113) Use examples from the text to support your impressions.

LEARNING FROM THE TEXT RESPONSE

What do you think of how children are treated at St. Peter's compared to your school? Would you still like to go to an English boarding school? Use examples from the text to support your impressions.

———

GROUP 3:

- Reread pages 119-121
  - Identify the CLIMAX in this section
- What language choices does Roald Dahl make to lead to this climactic moment?

CRITICAL STANCE RESPONSE

What were your impressions of the way the headmaster dealt with the punishment? (pg. 120) Use examples from the text to support your impressions.

LEARNING FROM THE TEXT RESPONSE

What do you think of how children are treated at St. Peter's compared to your school? Would you still like to go to an English boarding School? Use examples from the text to support your impressions.

Goat's Tobacco (TR)

Page Numbers/Chapters

Pgs.127-132, *Goat's Tobacco*

INITIAL UNDERSTANDING:

- Students share and discuss.
- Wonder Questions
- Big 6
- What is this story about?

LEARNING FROM THE TEXT:

Themes, social issues, and how the story changes the reader's perspective.

What does the chapter, *A Drive in the Motor Car*, teach us about how the time viewed masculinity? What does it mean to be "manly"?

DEVELOPING IDEAS:

Larger ideas, the big picture, what is happening, why it's happening, why and how characters act and do things.

- Why did Roald put the dried goat's poop in the manly lover's pipe?
- Why did the entire family approve of Roald making the "goat's tobacco"?

TAKING A CRITICAL STANCE:

Text's construction, language, effect on the reader, connections to other texts, perspective, writer's choice, powerful language, metaphors

- What did you expect when Dahl suggested that the manly lover "would have to suffer for it sooner or later"? (pg. 128) "It" is the fact that he took their sister away from them.

- What was your impression when the entire family seemed to approve of the "goat's tobacco" prank?
- What did you think of the way Dahl initially set up the image of the manly lover compared to the "not so manly" image of him after he breathed in the poopy smoke?
- How did you respond to the physical description of the manly lover's reaction to breathing in the smoke?
- BCR: Evaluate the effectiveness of Dahl's style of writing in telling his story(ies).

Exaggeration:

Throughout the chapter, the overemphasis on him being a "manly lover" (pg. 131), The manly lover's reaction to smoking the goat poop.

BCR Essay Author's Style (SR)

Boy, Tales of Childhood, pgs.127-132

Evaluate Dahl's writing style in telling the story of Goat's Tobacco. Use examples and details from the text to support your response.

BCR Grading Scale

20 – Answer the question with two clear, relevant examples and a meaningful extension/explanation.

17– Answer the question with two clear, relevant examples and a weak extension/explanation.

15– Answer the question with two clear, relevant examples.

13 – Answer the question with one clear, relevant example.

11– Answer the question

0– Response is completely incorrect, irrelevant to the question, or missing

Midway Theme Assignment (SR)

Directions: Think about every chapter that has been read up to this point. Are there any ideas, principles, and circumstances that seem to be recurring throughout the story? Identify at least two chapters that seem to cover similar ideas or principles. Then, explore the idea, principle, or circumstance using the guided questions.

Chapters:

1. Papa and Mama
2. Kindergarten
3. The Bicycle and the sweet-shop
5. The Great Mouse Plot
6. Mr. Coombes
7. Mrs. Pratchet's revenge
9. Going to Norway
10. The Magic Island
11. A visit to the doctor
12. First day
13. Writing home
14. The Matron
15. Homesickness
16. A drive in the motor-car
18. Captain Hardcastle
19. Little Ellis and the boil
20. Goat's tobacco

Recurring ideas, principles, and circumstances:

1. List two chapters that seem to present similar circumstances.

2. In no more than two sentences, write a summary of the conflict and resolution of the chapter listed for the first chapter.

3. In no more than two sentences, write a summary of the conflict and resolution of the chapter listed for the second chapter.

4. What principle or idea seems to be presenting itself in both chapters? (for example, honesty, relationships, making the right decision, etc.)

5. THEME: What does the reader learn about the principle or idea presented in both chapters? In other words, what broad idea, message, or moral can be applied to the reader's life through Roald Dahl's experience?

Theme BCR (SR)

Identify and explain one recurring theme in the novel. In your explanation, include what the reader can learn about life through Dahl's novel. Use examples and details from the text to support your response.

BCR Grading Scale

20 – Answer the question with two clear, relevant examples and a meaningful extension/explanation.

17– Answer the question with two clear, relevant examples and a weak extension/explanation.

15– Answer the question with two clear, relevant examples.

13 – Answer the question with one clear, relevant example.

11– Answer the question

0– Response is completely incorrect, irrelevant to the question, or missing

Getting dressed for the big school, Boazers, The Headmaster, Chocolates (TR)

Page Numbers/Chapters

Pgs.135-149, *Getting dressed for the big school, Boazers, The Headmaster, Chocolates*

INITIAL UNDERSTANDING:

- Students share and discuss.
- Wonder Questions
- Big 6
- What is this story about?

LEARNING FROM THE TEXT:

Themes, social issues, how the story changes the reader's perspective.

- What does the way English men dress suggest about the society in which this story takes place? (pg. 139)
- What does the story of the Headmaster at Repton suggest about how a person gains high positions of authority in society? (Pg. 144)

DEVELOPING IDEAS:

Larger ideas, the big picture, what is happening, why it's happening, why and how characters act and do things

- Why Dahl might have had to dress in such an elaborate outfit?
- Why were students only a few years older than the others allowed to punish younger students?
- Why wouldn't other people have known about the Repton headmaster's treatment to the boys?

• How can someone be so cruel in private yet appear so good in public?

• What caused Roald Dahl to dream such magnificent dreams while at Repton? (pg. 148)

TAKING A CRITICAL STANCE:

Text's construction, language, effect on the reader, connections to other texts, perspective, writer's choice, powerful language, and metaphors.

• The prefects at Repton are known as boazers. What does the term "boazer" suggest about their position?

• Which do you think is the cruellest of the three headmasters mentioned in the story (Mr. Coombes, St. Peter's, Repton)? Why?

• What were your impressions of Michael's beating from the Repton headmaster? (pg. 145)

• Do you think Dahl's doubts about God and religion were justifiable? (pg. 146)

• Based on what he said in the chapter *Chocolates*, how many other stories do you think Dahl wrote that were based on his experiences?

Reflective Details:

• pg. 138 – Dahl's thoughts on his uniform: "All this was bad enough..."

• pg. 144 – Dahl's thoughts on the Repton headmaster: "What is so interesting..."

• pgs. 144, 145 – Dahl's thoughts on why he laid so much emphasis on school beatings.

Point of View, Memory Details, Reflective Details (SR)

Throughout the novel, Roald Dahl uses **personal details** such as **memory details**, which come from his own experience and knowledge, and **reflective details**, which come from his own thoughts and feelings about the memory details. This use of **personal details** causes a shift of **point of view** throughout the novel – his perspective as a child and his perspective as an adult. Analyze a moment in the novel where **personal details** are used to show a **point of view** shift.

For example,

Childhood Perspective (memory detail)

I sat there gasping. The roof of my mouth seemed to be on fire. I grabbed my mother's hand and held on to it tight. I couldn't believe that anyone would do this to me (pg. 70).

Point of View:

How did Roald Dahl see the world as a child? He most likely felt betrayed and tricked by his parents and by the doctor because, without any kind of warning, the doctor inflicted terrible pain on him.

Adult Perspective (reflective detail)

That was in 1924, and taking out a child's adenoids, and often the tonsils as well, without any anesthetic was common practice in those days. I wonder, though, what you would think if some doctor did that to you today (pg. 71).

Point of View:

How does Roald Dahl see the world as an adult looking back on his childhood? He understands that this was necessary because of the lack of anesthetic. If he had been warned about the procedure, he would likely have fought the doctor during the operation.

Instructional Notes
- *Model the process with the examples above*
- *Select pages from the text best suited for the assignment*
- *Create a graphic organizer in two quadrants, one for the examples above and one for the student response.*

Point of View BCR (SR)

Identify a moment in the novel where Dahl uses point of view (as a child and as an adult) to tell the story and reflect upon the story. Explain the effect that these two perspectives have on the story.

BCR Grading Scale

20 – Answer the question with two clear, relevant examples and a meaningful extension/explanation.

17– Answer the question, two clear, relevant examples, weak extension/explanation.

15– Answer the question with two clear, relevant examples.

13 – Answer the question with one clear, relevant example.

11– Answer the question

0– Response is completely incorrect, irrelevant to the question, or missing

Corkers, Fagging, Games and photography, Goodbye school (TR)

Page Numbers/Chapters:

pgs.150-176, *Corkers, Fagging, Games and photography, Goodbye school*

INITIAL UNDERSTANDING:

- Students share and discuss.
- Wonder Questions
- Big 6
- What is this story about?

LEARNING FROM THE TEXT:

Themes, social issues, how the story changes the reader's perspective

- What does the chapter Corkers seem to suggest about the school system? The system of "Fagging" is a well-defined ritual allowed by the authorities in the school. What purpose might this serve in a boarding school?

- What does the need for the crème de la crème (pg. 167) and the type of work Dahl does (pg. 172, 175) seem to suggest about the Shell Company in the 1930s?

DEVELOPING IDEAS:

Larger ideas, the big picture, what is happening, why it's happening, why and how characters act and do things

- How do Corkers get away with pretending to teach the subject of mathematics?

- What would happen to Corkers and the rest of the class if he was caught?

- What would happen if a Fag ever refused the orders of a Boazer?

- Why are House Boazers allowed to make any Fag in the House do his bidding?

- What things might Dahl have done or said to make him unfit to be a Boazer? (pg. 162)

- Why wasn't getting into such schools as Oxford or Cambridge difficult?

TAKING A CRITICAL STANCE:

Text's construction, language, effect on the reader, connections to other texts, perspective, writer's choice, powerful language, metaphors

- In what way does the physical description of Corkers differ from the other adults Dahl has described? (i.e., Headmasters, Matron, Mrs. Pratchet, Capt. Hardcastle)

- Based on the description of "fagging," what does it mean to fag another person? What were your impressions of this practice?

- Which would you prefer? The life of a writer or the life of a businessman? (pg. 171)

Significant Character Relationship:

The student should be able to thoroughly discuss/explain the complexity of Dahl's relationship with his mother.

For further discussion:

What is the most important thing that Roald Dahl learned? Why is this so important?

Corkers to Goodbye School
Discussion Preparation (SR)

<u>Boy, Tales of Childhood</u>, pgs.150-176

Discussion Preparation 1

Answer each question on a loose-leaf piece of paper. Be prepared to share your response with the class.

Developing Ideas:

- How does Corkers get away with pretending to teach the subject of mathematics?

- What would happen to Corkers and the rest of the class if he was ever caught?

Learning from the text:

- What does the chapter *Corkers* seem to suggest about the school system? Use examples from the text to support your response.

Critical Stance (write in paragraph form)

- Who was the most important person in Roald Dahl's life? Support your answer with examples from the text.

- What was the most important lesson that Roald Dahl learned throughout his life as a child and as a young adult? Support your answer with examples from the text.

Discussion Preparation 2

Answer each question on a loose-leaf piece of paper. Be prepared to share your response with the class.

Developing Ideas:

• What would happen if a Fag ever refused the orders of a Boazer?

• Why are House Boazers allowed to make any Fag in the House do his bidding?

• What things might Dahl have done or said to make him unfit to be a Boazer? (pg. 162)

Learning from the text:

• Based on the description of "fagging," what does it mean to fag another person? What were your impressions of this practice?

Critical Stance (write in paragraph form)

• Who was the most important person in Roald Dahl's life? Support your answer with examples from the text.

• What was the most important lesson that Roald Dahl learned throughout his life as a child and as a young adult? Support your answer with examples from the text.

Discussion Preparation 3

Answer each question on a loose-leaf piece of paper. Be prepared to share your response with the class.

Developing Ideas:

• Why wasn't getting into such schools as Oxford or Cambridge difficult?

• Why does Dahl prefer to go to work rather than to go to Oxford or Cambridge?

• Why does Dahl desire to travel to foreign countries such as Africa?

Learning from the text:

• Which would you prefer? The life of a writer or the life of a businessman? (pg. 171)

Critical Stance (write in paragraph form)

• Who was the most important person in Roald Dahl's life? Support your answer with examples from the text.

• What was the most important lesson that Roald Dahl learned throughout his life as a child and as a young adult? Support your answer with examples from the text.

Plot Comparison (SR)

As you have already discovered through your examination of THEME, similar circumstances and experiences take place throughout the course of Roald Dahl's novel about his life. At this point, you will now examine two chapters in the novel for their basic plot structure.

First, review the plot elements and structures by labeling the three diagrams below.

Then, select two chapters that appear to share a similar basic plot structure. Then, draw the plot diagram that most accurately resembles the plot structure of each chapter. Finally, label the most important events of the plot on the plot diagram. Use a separate sheet of paper if needed.

FOLLOW-UP: What is the motivating purpose that drives both stories to their resolution?

About the Author

Tim, a seasoned educator with over 15 years of teaching experience across multiple grade levels in English and Drama, has established himself as a dedicated writer with a diverse academic background. He holds a B.S. in Theatre from Towson University, an M.A.T. from Notre Dame of Maryland University, and an M.A. in Creative Writing and Literature from Fairleigh Dickinson University.

Originally from Syracuse, New York, Tim currently resides in Maryland, where he imparts his passion for English, Creative Writing, Film, and Theatre to high school students. His journey into writing began earnestly in 2014, spurred by the encouragement of his own students.

Tim's love for storytelling stems from his upbringing, where his mother's dedication to reading to him and his siblings laid the foundation for his literary pursuits. Tim embarked on his writing endeavors, influenced by authors such as C. S. Lewis, J. R. R. Tolkien, Piers Anthony, and others in the mystery, thriller, and fantasy genres.

Since his debut publication in 2019, Tim has rapidly expanded his literary footprint, amassing a wealth of published works. Beyond writing, Tim enjoys indulging in his diverse interests, including reading, teaching, camping, savoring cigars, shooting, and attending live music concerts.

Follow Tim on Social Media

facebook.com/timothyrbaldwin

instagram.com/timothyrbaldwin

Read more at www.timothyrbaldwin.com.